Passing Your Real Estate Exam

15 Key Steps to passing the state requirements for entering the lucrative world of buying and selling property.

The Real Estate Industry is vast, with a solid history of investment, leaving it ripe for sales, construction and portfolio diversification.

In this forthright Itty Bitty® Book, Stephanie Stern shows you current and reliable key steps for passing your Real Estate Exam, thereby allowing you access to the tremendous wealth-generating world of Real Estate.

Those steps include:

- Understanding your personal learning style.
- Identifying and defining Real Estate terminology.
- Learning your state exam requirements.

If you are considering entering the world of Real Estate, pick up a copy of this valuable book today.

Your Amazing Itty Bitty® Real Estate Exam Book

15 Key Steps to PASSING Your Real Estate Exam With Flying Colors

Stephanie Stern

Published by Itty Bitty® Publishing
A subsidiary of S & P Productions, Inc.

Printed in the United States of America

Itty Bitty® Publishing
311 Main Street, Suite D
El Segundo, CA 90245
(310) 640-8885

ISBN: 978-0-9987597-7-7

To my wonderful husband, David; without you, there would be 'no me.' (How do you put up with me?)

Drop by our Itty Bitty® Publishing website to learn more about passing your real estate exam.

www.ittybittypublishing.com

Or share your thoughts at:
www.passingyourrealestateexam.com
#passingyourrealestateexam

Table of Contents

Introduction

Real Estate has changed my life. That change began by passing the Real Estate Exam.

Passing that exam was 'no joke' and a challenge. Sifting through all of the available information online including videos and podcasts, and even in classes, can be overwhelming, daunting and downright confusing. So I came up with a current and simple 15 steps to make it easier for you. Read, apply and enjoy the process! I'm sending you all of my very best for passing your real estate exam.

Move forward into action:

1. Identify your State's Requirements
2. Fulfill Preliminary Requirements
3. Learn the Material
4. Pass the Test

Step 1
Prepare Your State's Required Material

Before you can even apply to take your state's Real Estate Exam, you must take and pass a number of classes.

1. Real Estate Principles and Practices, together with an additional elective class, are usually the basic classes your state may require you to take.
2. The Real Estate elective class may be on Appraisal, Property Management, Real Estate Finance, Real Estate Economics, Escrows, etc.
3. Go here to access your state's Bureau of Real Estate website https://goo.gl/ZWhwQP and search for "Real Estate Exam Requirements."
4. Every state within the United States has prerequisite classes which must be satisfactorily completed in order to take that state's Real Estate Exam.
5. Research, at the library or online, the state where you are planning to do the greatest number of transactions (or the state where you live) to determine that state's exam requirements.

Get Started

After you identify which classes are required to be taken and passed before you are eligible to apply for the state exam, get started researching how to take them.

- There are many different venues at which to learn the material. These include, but are not limited to: Community Colleges or University Extension Programs, online classes, webinars or videos. You can also just get the books and read them yourself.
- Make sure to note if your state requires proof of class completion.

It's ok if you get confused or overwhelmed.

- There are so many ways to take the required classes. Choose the most convenient for you and your lifestyle.
- If one way isn't working out for you, you can always make another choice that is better and fits your personal learning style.

Step 2
Identify Your Learning Style

Auditory, Kinesthetic, Visual and Read/Writing are all learning styles. Focus on the best way for you to learn. It is imperative that you grasp what your learning style is.

1. Are you quick to recall something you've heard, read or done? Is writing it all down the strongest way for you to remember the information? Or are you someone that has to simply read the information in order to grasp the concepts? Whatever it is, that's great!
2. No single learning style is better than another. It's ok to have one or two or all of them that you identify with. However, if you really focus on it, I'm sure you'll find one that resonates with you. That's the one!
3. Begin searching out modalities that are best suited for your own personal style. When you know which one to use, you can then dive in to passing your real estate exam.

How to Identify Your Learning Style

There are tests you can take online and in books that will help you determine which is the best way for you to learn and comprehend new information.

- Search online what you think is your best way to learn.
- Go to your local library and check out a Learning Style book.
- Here is a list: https://goo.gl/YLhJGf

Step 3
Identify Current
Real Estate Terminology

Terminology is one of the most important things that real estate exams test for. It's like learning a new language.

1. Search online or your local library for 'Real Estate Terms.'
2. List all the terms on a sheet. Read them, memorize them and comprehend their meaning.
3. Here is a terminology list: https://goo.gl/fHk1LX

Real Estate Terms

Most of the terminology is not new; however, how the word or phrase is used in the sentence is. So when you memorize and understand the new terminology it will be much easier to pass your test.

- Keep all of the words and phrases together. It will be easier to comprehend them that way.
- Flashcards with Terms, Definitions and how the term can be used in a sentence will help.

Step 4
Set Your Schedule

Everyone has a life and life can have a tendency to get in the way of studying. So, it's vital to set your daily, weekly or hourly learning schedule.

1. Determine what time of day is ideal for your learning style.
2. It is important to set a regular time and if possible, a place for your study schedule and turn it into a habit.
3. No single schedule is better than another, the important thing is to get one and stick with it.

Setting Up Your Learning Schedule May Be Easier Than You Imagined

Try a schedule out for a week or two and make sure it is doable for you. If it doesn't work, try a different schedule until you find one that does. Here are a couple of things to consider:

- What time of day are you more alert?
- If you have a family, what hours are they out of the house, asleep or doing their own homework that will allow you time to study your material?
- How many hours can you devote to your learning?

Step 5
Begin Your Learning Process

You have identified what will be the easiest and most ideal learning environment for you to study for the exam. So, now it is time to implement your plan.

1. Start by enrolling in your class or classes.
2. Make sure you attend the classes, particularly if attendance is taken and passage is dependent on attendance.

Following Through May Be the Hardest Part

Take Action. You have done a lot of research identifying what you need to pass your Real Estate Exam; now it's time to do the work to pass.

- Take it one step at a time, one class at a time.
- Keep it simple. Don't overcomplicate it.

Step 6
Take Prep Tests

The prep tests can be found in the chapters of your Real Estate books.

Yes, they do help you. The terminology becomes more clear and this is where it all begins to really make sense.

1. Review your answers. Keeping a running total of your prep test answers are very helpful to measure your comprehension.
2. Your prep tests may be as close to your state's exam formatting as you can find. It was for me!

Prep Tests Really Are Helpful

- Take Real Estate prep tests online.
- Go here for some: https://goo.gl/HK2V6r
- Cross reference the ones from your books for relevancy.

Step 7
Breathe, Eat Healthily, Sleep, Exercise and Stop Perfectionism

You can get yourself stressed out by many things, especially when you want to pass a major test! The important thing to remember is to take the best possible care of yourself and stop trying to be perfect.

1. Deep breathing helps relieve stress and get your mind back on task.
2. A diet rich in vitamins, minerals and valuable nutrients will help to give your body the fuel it needs to pass this test.
3. 8-hours or more of sleep is extremely helpful. Your body and mind need to be able to retain the new information and apply it.
4. Moving your body throughout the day will increase blood flow and help your brain process this new real estate language.
5. Passing is good enough! Give yourself a break, a hug, some vital love by not trying to make 100%. Passing is the goal.

Being Kind to Yourself

- Relaxation exercises, meditation and mindfulness are tips to help you pass the test.
- Pat yourself on the back. You are doing a process some people only 'think about.' You are actually doing it…that's a big deal!

Step 8
Identify Where
The Test Will Be

Research your state's Real Estate Testing locations by going onto their website and looking for the testing site information.

1. Every state has a real estate website search area that lists where your testing site will be.
2. You can also use an internet search engine to explore the phrase, 'where is (your state's) Real Estate Exam Testing Site.'

There May Be More Than One Exam Site

If your state has multiple exam locations, then identify the one closest to you and the easiest for you to access.

- Use your zip code for a broader search.
- Use GPS, internet search or a map to get the best route for you.

Step 9
Identify Your State's
Application Process

Each state has a different process for applying.

1. Does your state have only one form to fill out? Find out on the examinee tab of their website.
2. Do they need a background check? If so, they usually offer information on how and where to apply for one.
3. Be honest. Disclose all prior history of any convictions or pending criminal charges.

Knowing Where to Look

Make sure you read and re-read the areas on their website for new Real Estate Licensees.

- Fill everything out legibly.
- Include any transcripts or completed course certificates.
- https://goo.gl/ZWhwQP

Step 10
Fill Out Required Paperwork

The application is only one part.

1. Your state may have you submit fingerprints through a third party.
2. They may have a payment form that must be mailed in.

Deadlines

Every form must be filled out and turned in on time.

- Deadline alarm. Set an alarm to make sure you don't miss the time to turn in your forms.
- Remember postage and mail times. Do not wait until the last minute to mail your applications. Life may have some delays that could make you miss your deadline.

Step 11
Send In Required Paperwork

Now that you have it filled out – send it in.

1. Check your state's website to learn how they want you to mail in your paperwork.

    a. USPS
    b. Fed Ex
    c. UPS

Online Submission

Check your state's Real Estate Exam website to see if you can submit your paperwork online. Here's a link to USA State Requirements: https://goo.gl/ZWhwQP

- Can you scan your paperwork and email it into your state's Real Estate Department?
- How about a .pdf version? Check out your state's Real Estate Exam website to make sure.

Step 12
Pay Required Fee(s)

Every state's Real Estate Exam website will tell you how much and which type of payment is required.

1. Send in a check by mail.
2. Pay by an online commerce site such as PayPal.

Payment Confirmation

After you make your required payment, make sure you receive a confirmation.

- Make a copy for yourself of all the paperwork you're submitting.
- Send by Certified Mail Return Receipt Requested.
- If paying online, take a screen shot from your computer screen of the payment completion.

Step 13
Continue The Learning Process

Remember to keep reading, learning and practicing.

1. Keep going! It's easy to stop and take a break. A small one is okay, a long one lasting for more than 2 days, is not.
2. You have almost completed the process. Review Steps 2 & 5, if need be.

Practice, Practice, Practice

Whatever your learning style is, keep doing it.

- Take time to read, watch and write your state's required material – before you go to sleep, upon awakening and during breaks. There is time to keep learning.

Step 14
Identify and Review
Your Weakest Areas

Practice test scores are a great way to see where you need more understanding of the material.

1. Your score is a good thing. It will tell you what areas of real estate to keep reviewing.
2. When your practice test score is consistently in the top passing percentile, you can be confident that you know that particular area and can move on to other areas of testing.

Three or More Times

Consistently scoring 100% or close to that on your practice tests three or more times in a row means you can probably move on to other areas of your state's required Real Estate Exam material.

- Keep track of how many times you've taken a specific test.
- Write down your scores in a ledger so you can track the information easily.

Step 15
Show Up Early, Follow All Verbal and Written Instructions

It's arrived! The time has come for you to pass your Real Estate Exam. You're going to do this!

1. Arrive at least ten minutes early. Walk around the test site before checking in.
2. Go to the restroom BEFORE you check in.
3. Ask before you check in if you are allowed to leave the testing site once you begin, in case you need a quick break.

Be Kind to The Testing Staff

They are there to help you. Listen to what they say and follow their instructions.

- Check in politely.
- Check out politely.

When you get your results, remember, others may not have passed. Be considerate of that.

Now, go congratulate yourself for PASSING YOUR REAL ESTATE EXAM!!

You've finished. Before you go…

Share that you finished this book.

Please star rate this book.

Reviews are solid gold to writers. Please take a few minutes to give us some itty bitty feedback.

ABOUT THE AUTHOR

Stephanie Stern loves all facets of the Real Estate Industry. She has experience with many different areas such as Construction, Tenant Improvements, Project Management, Sales, Marketing and Investments for Residential, as well as, Commercial. She lives in Los Angeles with her fabulous husband, David, and dreams of having many animals, old and young, to love on.

You can reach Stephanie at:
www.passingyourrealestateexam.com

If you enjoyed this Itty Bitty® Book, you might also enjoy the following:

- **Your Amazing Itty Bitty® Self Esteem Book** – Jade Elizabeth

- **Your Amazing Itty Bitty® Message Mastery Book – Sarah Coolidge**

- **Your Amazing Itty Bitty® Mastering The Back Office Book** – Karen O'Connor

And many other Itty Bitty® Books available online.

www.ingramcontent.com/pod-product-compliance
Lightning Source LLC
Chambersburg PA
CBHW071422200326
41520CB00014B/3538